SPARKS *of the* *Season*

- VITAL SIGNS OF COMFORT AND JOY -

Under God's Wings

JUDY IMRIE

Tellwell Talent
www.tellwell.ca

ISBN
978-0-2288-4249-1 (Hardcover)
978-0-2288-4248-4 (Paperback)
978-0-2288-4250-7 (eBook)

IN DEDICATION AND MEMORY OF

'THE SPARKS'

SARA-DYAN CROSS
WILLIAM (BILL) HERON
JOYCE ELLERY
ROSALIE EDGAR

And all the other 'Sparks' who have carried light into
the shadows of our world.

"UNTIL THEN"

SPARKS OF THE SEASON
Vital Signs of Comfort and Joy

Table of Contents

Preface vii

Ember 1

The Last Day of Christmas 3
The Glass Ceiling 8

Ember 2

Whispering Woods 13

Ember 3

The Offering.. 23
The Christmas of the Missing Joseph........................... 26
My Lady in Stone.. 29
All I Want for Christmas.. 30
The Manger in the Window... 33

Ember 4

Sparks of the Season.. 37
Sara's Spark 40
Transition.. 48

Ember 5

Epiphany.. 53
Epilogue.. 57
Star 59
Wisdom 60
Aftermath 61
Rogue Wave 64
Author's Note.. 65
About The Author.. 71

One ember glowing in the dark
To spark ten thousand candle flames.

Preface

"Signed, sealed, delivered..." That old song circles through my mind. I am finally committing, to paper at least, random thoughts involving this strange Advent and Christmas season. There has been much coming and going in more ways than one. I suppose, at the age of 71, I can expect 'four funerals and no weddings' in the space of as many weeks, two prohibited by weather to even attend. The services were conducted in four different traditions — Pentecostal, Anglican, Salvation Army, and Baptist — but grief is grief. It levels us all...at least for a time.

Today is February 2nd, remembered as Candlemas. This marks the day when Jesus was presented to the temple according to custom, with all the untested parental pride surrounding firstborn infants. Yearly, I keep a few treasured Christmas ornaments out on display until now...silver snowflakes on the windows, a miniature village glistening in sugar snow, and all the manger scenes before packing them away... all but one. I hold on tightly to seasons, savouring the sparks, the embers of joy, to warm the dark winter nights.

On this day, as my thoughts begin to gather, perhaps I too shall bring this lesser offering to the world. Dare I sign, seal, and deliver it also, maybe you will read it. May it bring Comfort and Joy.

Ember 1

"And the sea coast shall be dwellings
and cottages for shepherds
and folds for flocks."

Zephaniah 2:6
King James Version

- THE LAST DAY OF CHRISTMAS -
- THE GLASS CEILING -

THE LAST DAY OF CHRISTMAS

Traditionally, this is when it all comes together…a plethora of leaping lords, milking maids, golden rings. This one was very different. It was instead a subtraction, a taking away. The day before, the news came. 'Next-Door Rosalie,' cousin and friend, part of the Sisterhood of the Travelling Turkeys, would be leaving…not just the cottages on our beloved lake, not just 20 years of shared summers, but for always. After a shocking diagnosis in October, all treatment was ended. She had entered the same hospice from which I had watched my mother prepare to leave this Earth.

My day had moved on in its usual pattern, with my husband and me treated at the end of the day to dinner with an old friend. Just after, as we settled in for the evening, the phone rang. It could not have happened so fast. This was only Sunday. Two hours away, we had planned to visit Rosalie on Wednesday. It was not the first such call of this season. Thankfully, it would prove to be the last.

Later, Susan, friend and Priest-In-Charge of our little Anglican church, posed a question. What did all these deaths mean to me, coming so close together, all through Advent and Christmas? Perhaps, in the jotting down of my solo notes, I will hear the singing of some distant angel, somehow harmonize with heaven.

First, there are others to attend to. I sit down, not with a harp but a Chrome book, and began a letter to Rosalie's granddaughters. What can I possibly say to Eve and Livy? Rosalie was a quintessential grandmother: host of scavenger hunts at the cottage and tea parties on the deck, complete with fancy hats; encourager at all of their sports events; constant chauffeur; gentle protector. Even away from the lake, with living on adjacent farms she was always beside them. Where do I start? With a story, of course…where every grandmother begins.

February 5th, 2020

Dear Eve and Livy:

January 5th 2020, this 12th day of Christmas, will remain stored in your memory. That morning, unaware of what was about to unfold, I turned the tree lights on for the last time. As I walked away, my eye caught its entire image reflected in the window. All the glory of Christmas appeared to be standing on the outside. A memory came back of my grandmother who I had never known on this Earth.

She died when my mother was only seven. Every August I think of the day when Mom was taken into town to say her goodbyes and how difficult that must have been. She was staying with your great-great-grandparents, on the farm bordering the lake, the place your grandmother would later call home. Every time I thought of my own grandmother, there was a void, a sadness. Her life had not been an easy one for many reasons.

Many years later, our family was sitting in the church back home, waiting for one more wedding to begin. Out of the blue, in the midst of this jovial crowd, I was jolted by a surprise, astonished, then satisfied. Beyond explanation, the Presence of Joy simply enfolded me. Through the matrix of that Joy, my grandmother came.

I had not conjured up that moment nor do I have any inclination to visit mediums or attend séances. There were no visuals or sounds, just a knowing, a meeting of her true self. It felt like my hand was on one side of a glass window and her hand was on the other. There came a deep assurance that she was happy and present with all of us. I was never to remember her in sadness again and I never have.

I went off to church as usual on this last day of Christmas. Held in the sweet familiar, the words of the Communion Service[1] fell softly, softly into my mind, etching images of places where crossover happens; a tear appears in the thin veil dividing this world and heaven. Stretching to open, the timelessness of eternity pours into time itself. A dividing wall of water breaks, the singing begins. God slips in… the Saviour comes. A birthing, not a dying. Little did I know the

---

[1] *Personal paraphrased reflections inspired by Eucharistic Prayer for Christmas Seasons of The Spirit. Wood Lake Publishing Inc.*

phone call that was also coming, and the number of hearts that would break that day.

Your grandmother first opened her cottage up to us for vacations 20 years ago. Then, one magical day, next-door 'Witz End' came up for sale. Oh, the joy! Twenty years of watching the sunrise crack open another hot summer day over our beloved lake, its beams dancing on the coolness of its surface until the holy hour at dusk when the water turns to lavender silver. Twenty years of summer…

Always she was there, your grandmother, unless she was off on some frequent mission. She will be still, cheering from the rafters, urging you headlong into whatever adventures lie ahead for both of you. Her hand is pressed against the window of heaven, which will open one day in welcome. She is there behind every 'glass ceiling' the two of you will ever break, echoing "Last one in is a rotten egg" from the docks of each new plunge.

In the meantime, sometimes, the tears come, the anger burns. I can't imagine there will be no more 'Rosalie stories'…no more chats over the fence…the cottage is tinged now with sadness, and even the memories bring pain, but all of hers have turned to praise and all of ours will too…praise for having had this extraordinary, hilarious, compassionate person in our lives, now carried in our hearts.

Rosalie and I may not have been part of 'The Sisterhood of the Travelling Pants' but we were members of 'The Sisterhood of The Travelling Turkeys.' Often we'd catch each other driving cooked turkeys to various family events. She will come back in memory with each scent of this succulent holiday food. The laughter and the love have not gone away.

My favourite picture hangs framed in the side entrance of our home. I have passed it hundreds of times, coming and going. It shows all four of our grandchildren sitting on the couch in 'Rosalie Cottage.' Clad in their latest cartoon character pyjamas, showing off eight bare feet, they sit sealed in some endless summer morning… Cottage Kids, Stepping Stones glued together… Ashton, 'The Elder' at seven, only- granddaughter-in-charge; and Nathan, the youngest at three; both book ended by Nicholas and Chase. Heads thrown back in laughter, I can hear them still. This joy, this happiness, your grandmother gave to so many of us…most of all, to both of you. May that joy grow greater each day than the sorrow you endure now.

Much love. See you on the dock. Remember this:

THE GLASS CEILING

The tree lights glowed into the window of the room,
Slipped through the pane of glass
Crossovered to the other side,
Blazing in Glory.
And she, she too slipped from our lives,
Took with herself such laughter,
Such beauty,
All that ever she was…
Crossovered.
Slipped through the pain of life,
Crossovered to the other side…
Shattering death in her wake.

Judy

Cottage Kids

From left to right; Nicholas, Ashton, Nathan, Chase

Ember 2

"For you shall go out with joy and be led out with peace:
the mountains and the hills shall break forth into
singing.
and all the trees of the field shall clap their hands."

Isaiah 55:12
The New King James Version

- WHISPERING WOODS-

WHISPERING WOODS

Later, folding this letter, I thought for a moment of other shining Christmas trees, other times, allowing my mind to slip back into a comforting place, far away and long ago...

The first Christmas sealed in my memory, now crumbling somewhat around the edges, must have been the year I was three. No siblings had entered my universe as yet and I was, according to myself, the centre of my parents' life. I recall that pine-sweet, magical morning of descending the stairs in my padded-feet pyjamas, feeling reality slip away. Apparently, I uttered the words, "Oh my stars..." — never said before nor since that I know of — for under our Sparkling Tree, magic waited. A dove-grey baby carriage with a leatherette retractable hood contained the biggest, most beautiful baby doll on Earth.

My brother, Paul, would arrive the next August and I was a reluctant big sister, but this Christmas gift, dropped from the skies, made me a forever devoted follower of St. Nicholas. He became my patron saint. Fifty years later, this gift would only be topped by the birth of our first-born grandson on The Eve of Christmas. Besides Jesus Himself, our very own Nicholas was the best Christmas gift ever.

When I had grown up, my mother made a confession. My dad had worked overtime for three months in order to buy such an extravagant gift. This in no way dampened my trust in St. Nicholas, nudging humans behind the scenes. If only we would listen, there is such a spirit of generosity abroad with more than enough for all.

My father had known Depression Christmases as a boy, including the loss of the family farm. This would end his formal education at the age of 11, sending him out to work as a 'hired hand.' This left him with an inbred loneliness, and a determination that his children would never know such a bleak time. My father's sacrifice, untouched by the commercial, left me with a lifetime of enjoyment, buying, wrapping, and surprising others as I had been. Years later, my husband would double this original joy by having my doll carriage refurbished. It remains in our living room to this day.

Childhood Christmases flowed together, very much the same, and that is exactly what I loved about them. Two sisters, Maureen and Cheryl, were added over the years and it was my delight to engage their talents, along with our brother, for the Christmas Eve Play.

Memories differ on this score but, apparently, I directed, starred, and provided the angelic musical numbers for each performance. My siblings were relegated to roaming around with tea towels stuck on their heads —apparently, not very happily. (The original shepherds probably weren't either, combining the cold, a blast of angel choirs, and possibly a stampede of terrified sheep.)

During one such extravaganza, a phone call was placed to the only hardware store in town where my uncle was working the evening shift. This was an attempt to include him in my piano recital. I can still imagine the notes of Silent Night, gently wafting over him as the line of harried last-minute shoppers grew…men in their natural habitat buying toasters for their wives. Always remembered, never repeated.

We lived beside a double house that was home to two younger aunts, two older 'greats,' and one uncle. Aunt Maude 'with an E' (not to be confused with Great-Aunt Maud 'without an E') was simply called 'Maudie.' Probably part elf, the festivities of Christmas Eve began when she arrived with her treasure trove of homemade gifts. This took more than one trip.

I still have my felt apron depicting Dale Evans wearing her Kurly Kate pot-scrubber hair. (I never did get my long-desired pony, but that apron was a close second.) Crafty Maudie turned out such delights as my scarlet corduroy stuffed dog wearing a festive rhinestone collar and my rose sequined hat, scarf, and purse set whipped up on the old Singer sewing machine. There were plaster of Paris Santa Clauses, first set in red moulds before being hand-painted. One of these still stands on a shelf at our cottage. They appeared a long side fantastical candles for the Christmas Table, never to meet with a match. Not a battery in sight but we loved it all. If only all children were so blessed.

Never one to waste a penny in Elf Land, Maudie once set an old clogged can of spray snow in a pot of boiling water. (Don't try this at home.) Mercifully, the exploding contents only covered her glasses, plastering them in a vision of white. 'Angry Elf' assumed she had been blinded, and why she wasn't surely must have been left in the hands of some guardian Christmas angel hovering over The Workshop.

I also loved to savour the first moments of Christmas morning. Our stockings grew as we did into brown shopping bags seasonally decorated the night before. There is no feeling in the world like seeing them, stuffed to the brim, perched on the end of our beds. Slowly, slowly I would open each treasure, never wanting it to end.

My siblings' approach was an early morning Rip and Tear Event, but we weren't allowed to descend to The Tree until all the 'stockings' were emptied. My savouring therefore was pure torture for the others, forced next to line up on the staircase and just 'View The Tree.' I loved that part with the anticipation of countless treasures awaiting our arrival under the glowing branches. One sister swears she could smell the rubber head of her new doll clear across the living room.

The Tree was not some well-proportioned beauty bought from a lot. Oh no. Two weeks before The Day, we four and Dad had trekked miles across the frozen tundra to find the Annual Woodland Giant. In memory, it was always a perfect winter day. There, we hacked down the biggest, most beautiful specimen the forest had to offer…

at least it looked that way, covered with snow. Best of all, we had our busy father all to ourselves and that was part of the magic. A few weeks after his January death, many years later, these memories all came back, released from the Place of Long Ago, guarded in the heart.

THE WHISPERING WOODS

Once upon a golden time when Santa
Claus and stars were mine,
Two weeks before the magic day…
My dad would take us out to play.

We trudged, dwarf-like, hi-ho, hi-ho
Set to work and off we'd go.
(My mother probably danced a jig
When Dad would load us in the rig.)

Then deep into the woods we'd go…
My heart, it always seemed to know
The trees were whispering secret things
In language only angels sing.

And when the treasure trove was found
We'd cut and lift and drag to town
Cross the forest's snowy plain
The gift of silence, sun, and rain.

No house could hold The Woodland Giant
But Dad with axe was quite defiant.
There at the end of that pine-sweet day
A room transfigured, hallowed, lay.

The lights would fizzle, fade, then glow
Cause Dad would always seem to know

What bulb to change, what wire to tap
And then we'd fill in all the gaps…
As high as we could throw.

The Tinsel War was always fought.
Each year brother would be caught
Hurling it with blizzard force
Instead of hanging it of course…
With sister's symmetry.

Yet on the eve of this awesome quest
With sunset swallowed in the west,
Time transcended into space…
Leaving us in captured grace…
In the shimmering light of the Christmas Tree
The angels had come home with me.

Life happened as it always does
And I decided, in the fuss
Of 50 Christmases to my name,
I would not go to the woods again.

That year, my parents could not come.
The next, my father had succumbed
To a stroke and would not bring
The Silent Giant Woodland King.

But then a tiny cry was heard
And magic deep within me stirred.
My grandson Nicholas, came instead
To fill my empty manger bed.

He bathed in the light of the golden smile,
Ashton Mikayla's, our Lady Child…
And now another one is due
Who hears the singing angels too.

The circle widens, cousins come,
Another merry band begun
To find their Silent Woodland Giant
Asleep in snows where all is quiet.

Still I 'go' to the woods again,
Cross the snowy forest plain.
Santa Claus and stars are mine
For in Dad's footsteps, we all climb
Laughing as we go.

In silvered space, a silence falls.
The ancient woods to my spirit calls.
The wind, it whispers as we trace
The dear, familiar childhood pace…
"In deeper woods than you can find,
In sweeter joy beyond all time.
You only see the frozen sod;
Your father's heart is held in God's."

In the whispering hollow of this land
My father dwells in God's own hand.
Now I know the angels' song…
Our lives are carved upon God's palm.

Ember 3

"The sacrifices of God are a broken spirit:
a broken and a contrite heart
O God,
You will not despise.

He shall regard the prayer of the destitute,
and not despise their prayer."

Psalm 51:17
Psalm 102:17
The New King James Version

- THE OFFERING -
- THE CHRISTMAS OF THE MISSING JOSEPH -
-MY LADY IN STONE -
-ALL I WANT FOR CHRISTMAS -
- THE MANGER IN THE WINDOW-

THE OFFERING

Our childhood home, built by ancestors, was a large, forever-rambling three-storey house. More than a little frayed around the edges and stable-cold on December nights, the front door opened into a panelled foyer featuring two rounded wooden pillars dividing it from the living room.

At the bottom of its winding staircase, a stained-glass window provided one of the last remaining traces of elegance against which to feature the Manger Scene. I loved the stolen quiet moments before climbing those 'Jacob ladder' stairs to bed. One might also encounter angels, pausing to peer into The Holy.

This Nativity was just a cardboard set my parents had had forever which would later pass to me. Then, slowly, over time, I began adding miniature mementos in front of its familiar figures such as bits and pieces from family trips with my husband, Jerry, and daughters, Jennifer and Shannon. It helped to bring the memory of each year's travels or events into the Grand Finale and somehow drew me into the everyday life of this miraculous story.

Once, amid such treasures, a tiny gorilla was added, staring from a bonsai tree, just to the right of an adoring Mary. This marks in memory the year Daughter Number

2 decided she would like to grace the Sunday School Nativity play as that amazing creature. Shannon eventually agreed to be a lamb but retained the heart of those noble beasts. (That concert was almost as much fun as another one when Chicken Pox 'Came to Town' ahead of Santa Claus putting both Wise Men and Shepherds to bed.)

One carolling session turned disastrous too. We, the Women of the Mothers' Union, referred to by one husband as The Mothers' Onion, decided to serenade the new moms of the village. Combine a cold night, some giggling between houses, and one weak bladder and you can imagine the rest all by yourself. Suffice it to say, I returned to our farmhouse that evening in another caroller's borrowed underwear and a pair of her teenage son's camouflage pants. Typically, my husband-behind-a-newspaper never noticed a thing. However, in the morning, our teenage daughters were mortified. Always remembered, never repeated.

Our little country church once featured numerous Manger Scenes put on display during Advent. (This was much easier than pageants.) Off I trotted, a little apprehensive about my unique Bethlehem rendition gathered over the years. Actually, it got the most attention, at least for imagination. This explanatory poem was attached simply entitled:

THE OFFERING

Lord Jesus, every year, before Your infant smile,
I lay the woolly lambs,
This snow-white ram,
The carved brown owl…

But also, Lord, I bring, a feathered pink flamingo,
A red and yellow parrot,
One shiny orange turtle
Reminding me of happy days beneath a tropic sun.

A straw doll leads a goose of spicy tamarac
Causing golden memories to come all tumbling back.

A Christmas mouse and Rudolf
Adorn your stable bare
And from a bonsai tree, a brown gorilla stares.

Then before your manger coarse
I place a tiny rocking horse,
One black wool lamb,
A teddy bear…

I bring these Lord,
I dare, I dare because You give
The Unexpected Joy!
Pink flamingos, orange turtles, spicey tamarack…

I give, I give, what You have given, back!

THE CHRISTMAS OF
THE MISSING JOSEPH

If only life had stayed so simple. A much later Christmas Season found me searching for the perfect gift for one of our daughters. The ending of a marriage is a grief like no other and life would be forever changed, especially for their four-year-old daughter and 15-month-old son.

That year found me roaming around a favourite antique and gift shop when I spied a beautiful, Renaissance-appearing Manger Scene. The price was prohibitive but, following a St. Nicholas Nudge, I roamed into the back rooms. My knee struck a small table, causing me to look down. There it was, an identical set, half-price. I rushed my treasure to the front and, in my haste, asked why it was on sale. "Joseph is Missing," the clerk responded. This year the 'memento' would be an empty space.

On Christmas Eve, my husband and I settled in for the night with this depleted little family. The Day was muted in spite of the joy children always bring. I kept glancing at that Manger Scene. Mary was still there, the Shepherds, the Wise Men, all in place. Jesus remained. So much had been lost but so much was left. One could almost imagine, in a modern setting, that Joseph had just slipped out for diapers.

That Christmas became 'The Christmas of the Missing Joseph.' It was not the merriest but it was a peaceful oasis in a stormy time. Life went on. The grandchildren are now in their twenties, active and engaged in their lives which 'Joseph' has remained part of. Our family grew to include another son-in-law who has stayed faithfully through thick and thin. Some sorrows never go completely away but joy is greater. Perspective grows with gratitude.

Years before, I had encountered a living Madonna and Child. When our girls were still teenagers, we took a vote on where we would like to go for a family vacation. Result: Amsterdam 1. Mexico 3. Reluctantly, I bowed to the democratic decision. Perhaps I would pass through Anne Frank's House some other time. Instead, I would catch a glimpse of the suffering of another.

We are travelling through that ancient city in Mexico, any city, with a tour guide. On a stretch of road, a statue the colour of sand comes into view. Motionless, her head is cast down under a shawl. One hand holds a begging bowl, another shelters her silent child. Suddenly, encased in dust, she moves.

Face to face, shocked and speechless, my mind photographs that moment, stores it away until it comes flashing back. Sometimes since, I have wondered if this mother and child were not part of some shimmering mirage caught in the heat of the day… a dreamscape, etched in time, demanding at last to be noticed.

Weeks later, searching for gifts back home, I come upon a statue the colour of sand. It is shaped like a pillar topped with only an emerging head, balancing a begging bowl. She is there again… 'My Lady in Stone.' Stars float in front of my eyes as the memory explodes. This Madonna and Child, no longer frozen in time, blaze back, thawing my heart. Who are they? What is their story? Why am I remembering this family I have never known? Later, these words would arrive:

MY LADY IN STONE

All that morning, Jose, or was it Antonio,
with the face of an angel
Drove us through the city streets.

Through fractured Spanish/English,
Charades of signs and smiles,
We began to love his Mexico.

I didn't want to see her but knew that I would.
Baked into stone with her begging bowl,
Dragging her child behind her.

Even now, still she comes, like a sudden flash in
A mushroom cloud
Deafening in her silence.

Baked into stone, she cannot speak;
Seared on my heart she can.

Even now, still she comes,
Bearing my face in the looking glass.

She cannot speak;

I can.

ALL I WANT FOR CHRISTMAS

After extolling the wonders of the Christmas season to a friend, a single mom of several children, she groaned and said, "Just wake me up when the donkey stops." Obviously, her experiences of this 'happiest time of the year' weren't measuring up to mine. As the magic bubble of childhood pops, leaving behind the real world, the shape of Christmas changes and we accommodate, as humans do, but the longing for that perfect time haunts all of us, whether we have ever known it or not.

One by one, my brother, my sisters, and me left the rambling family home, long passed into other hands. Our parents and all the aunts and uncle of next door, including The Elf, have departed. We are blessed to still occasionally gather with siblings, children, and grandchildren but always I am pulled back in longing, looking ahead in wonder.

Even though it was years ago when I packed two anxious little ones into their father's vehicle, I can still feel the tiny hand of my granddaughter grabbing my arm; I can hear her voice saying, "Stay with me, Nana, till Daddy comes back." They had just become part of the ever-growing legion of Suitcase Children spanning the distance between two households. Their dad had disappeared into my daughter's home for a moment to retrieve some forgotten item and my grandchildren were in 'the no man's land of the changeover.'

Later, I would put my pain and theirs to paper, but we had landed on the dark side of the moon and I could find no way out. This was a very different Christmas territory and I wasn't sure if even St. Nicholas could find us there. All I wanted for Christmas could never be boxed and wrapped and placed under some shining tree. I wrote a letter to him anyway:

> However scattered or far apart, there
> dwells a prayer within my heart
> That on some shiny, Christmas Day,
> none of us will be away.
> But all our stresses and all our fuss can
> never make that true for us.
> And yet a deeper path we find because we trust that in
> God's time
> The gate will open to a place
> Prepared for us, all wrapped in grace.

> There deeper still a Banqueting Hall,
> With no one missing, none at all.

"No one missing, none at all," remains the deepest heart's cry of the season, yet death, separation, divorce, family feuds, and poverty play no favourites. Often, it is not 'the happiest time of the year.' Indeed, it can be the saddest. In so many hearts there is always that longing for someone or something lost; Earth simply cannot provide…all the

Missing Josephs of our lives. We mourn for that elusive Perfect Christmas — if not for ourselves, for those we love...

Next Year...Next Year...

THE MANGER IN
THE WINDOW

Before the late rising December sun makes its languid appearance, I sit in my dining room, curled up in a corner of the love seat. There is a manger scene in the window that never gets packed away, illuminated now by candlelight. It is all in one piece and beautifully detailed, drawing me into this quiet hour before the chaos begins. Jet-lagged from a November visit with family in England, I am way behind in preparations for the coming season. Rosalie's diagnosis and the pressing needs of others begin to crowd into my mind. My prayer list is endless. Once again, I scribble my pain on paper:

"The requests come like shards of broken glass grating against my heart. Too much... too deep... I cannot move for the pain yet still my breathing comes…life remains in this November of my soul. I kneel before the Holy Family, caught in the rays of candlelight. Words also come with whispered names released into the air. The Word Himself dawns in flaming light. God is here. My God is here.

> In the stable of our hearts keep us quiet;
> In the manger of our souls, keep us still.
> Come quickly, Lord Jesus, into this moment,
> Come soon into this now, Emmanuel.
> In the stable of our hearts, keep us quiet;

In the manger of our souls, keep us still.
Come quickly, Lord Jesus,
Into this moment,
Cover us beneath the healing of Your wings."

The Essence of the Presence slips into the room, enfolding me, answering this prayer through the next difficult days of Advent, of Christmas… in ways I had never asked nor expected. The next morning, on the official birthday of St. Nicholas, the first phone call came.

Ember 4

"The righteous shall flourish like
a palm tree: he shall grow
like a cedar in Lebanon
Those that be planted in the house of the Lord
shall flourish in the courts of our God."

Psalm 92:12,13
King James Version

- SPARKS OF THE SEASON -
- SARA'S SPARK-
-TRANSITION-

SPARKS OF THE SEASON

-SARA-DYAN-

Randomly, you sit beside someone you have never met before and will never see again, at least not on this Earth. Their presence some how stays with you, embedding traces of a kindred soul upon your own. Such is the memory of a chance encounter at a bridal shower I have of Sara-Dyan. I still remember her as a teenager with dark curly hair, merry eyes, outstanding personality. Her grandfather was the pastor at my sister Maureen's church. It stands on a property bordering the lake, the same one we all grew up beside.

Often my sister and I give each other prayer requests; years ago, one of hers came in for Sara-Dyan. It was heartbreaking news. This vibrant, beautiful young girl had just received a devastating diagnosis...a genetic disorder that would rob her over the years of eyesight, intellect, movement, dignity itself — everything, that is, except this deep love she had for Jesus. She wore a necklace bearing His Name engraved in Braille on a small charm. Her deepest desire was for everyone to enjoy the same relationship she had with Him.

Under God's grace and strength, her family's abiding love and care, coupled with her own indomitable spirit,

Sara-Dyan lived well beyond her normal expected span. Beneath crushing odds, they all carried the weight of seemingly unanswered faith with courage. At the age of 33, on this December 6, 2019, Sara-Dyan quietly slipped away into The Presence.

"Jesus, where have You been in all of this? Where indeed?" my smaller faith asks. "What is this all about... this joy, this heartbreak?"

"It is well with the child. It is well with the child," the silent whisper comes. Could it be…could it be…what lies ahead is so amazing, so astonishing, we will have forgotten even the question?

As plans for the funeral unfold, my sister and I talk often. Sara-Dyan has been a big part of her and her family's life and she feels the loss deeply. One of Maureen's unique ministries is to create memorial Christmas wreaths for anyone in the church who has suffered the loss of a loved one. Beautifully decorated, they contain miniature ornaments relating to the lives that have been lived. Sara-Dyan's is already begun with a purple ribbon for royalty, the favourite colour of this girl whose name means 'Princess.' So far there is an angel, a tiny Anne of Green Gables doll, and one butterfly — the simple, heartbreaking reminders of her life.

From my sister's craft box, two strands of thickened thread, white with green sparkles, fall to the floor. They are reminiscent of DNA. Maureen struggles to add these bits to the wreath. One weaves in perfectly. The other has a kink in it and would not flow right. She puts this piece at the bottom of the wreath to hide the defect.

As she hangs the finished wreath on the wall, it begins to fall but she catches it in both hands. In the darkened room, there is a sudden flash of a spark and Maureen notices that the bottom awkward strand has not only moved up but is solidly joined with the other strand, forming a cross at the junction. There is no explaining some things that happen at Christmas or anytime. Sara's-Dyan's last name is 'Cross.'

I have not inherited The Maudie Gene, as my sister has, but we all have our gifts and Maureen casually mentions perhaps I could write a poem for Sara. No pressure, of course, but I know my sister well. Usually I balk at such suggestions. I don't choose to write poems. The poems choose to come to me, often at awkward times. They are scribbled on the back of envelopes, grocery lists — whatever is at hand.

That night, I sit down in front of my Christmas tree. A picture forms in my mind of the interior of Sara-Dyan's church. It is evening. My eyes scan an audience of faces, each illuminated by candlelight. A large choir fills the stage. A dark-haired girl, as I remember her, is among the singers. Holy, Holy, Holy. Words begin to flow, few and sweet. Her family graciously decides to incorporate them into Sara-Dyan's funeral bulletin... whispers from heaven, printed in purple.

Maureen has another friend, skilled in jewellery-making, who creates purple resin heart-shaped necklaces. These are keepsakes for Sara-Dyan's mother, sister, aunts, etc. to wear at the funeral. There are sparkles in the resin. I am also given one, now worn attached to my tiny silver cross. Every now and then, caught in a ray of light, it reminds me of her:

SARA'S SPARK

Through braided strands of DNA
She came to us…a priceless gift.
With earthly eyes we
could not see
The blessing she was meant to be…
One ember glowing in the dark
To spark ten thousand candle flames.

Sara-Dyan Cross

-BILL-

December 23rd, 2019, 3:00 p.m., Pearson International Airport…we are gathered at the gate of arrivals, waiting for Nicholas, this time not to be born, but to arrive home for Christmas from a term at Manheim University in Germany.

He will be 20 tomorrow: tall, dark, handsome, brilliant, dearly loved. Tianna, his tiny nursing student girlfriend of many years, stands with us: mother Shannon and grandmother me. Anxiously, we scour the board to see who has landed. It is the busiest airport day of the year for what appears to be thousands of arrivals walking into the waiting arms of family. Echoes of heaven. Is this what it will be like?

One hilarious, large woman bombs out in front of us, opens her arms, and shouts: "Are you all waiting for me!? I'm here!!" Another passenger scurries shyly by, dressed in a unicorn onesie. There is 'Always One'… or two, obviously. She gets a round of applause as well from the Christmas-giddy crowd.

The wait goes on and on and suddenly, there he is, OUR boy, now 6'5", slightly bedraggled in sweatpants. His luggage will spend Christmas in Dublin, but our Nicholas is home. Oh, the joy! Soon he is mowing down on Canadian restaurant food once again, now joined by our faithful chauffeur, his Popa. Soon they have begun their traditional argument over which National Hockey Team is best. Sweet normal.

Earlier that day, we spent time with another family whose lives will never be normal again. They had not been for a very long time. Never before have I attended a funeral for someone I did not know, but by the end of this one, I so wished that I had.

Bill was the dearly loved brother of one of Shannon's university roommates. Like Sara-Dyan, he also entered this world where he would find much to overcome. His heart was already badly compromised at birth and required multiple surgeries, his hands were formed differently, yet this truly remarkable young man became a space engineer, taught others how to sail, and married a brilliant classmate. Together, they brought two compassionate, talented children into the world. He also died at 44 years of age.

The words of his mother's poignant eulogy still ring in my ears: "Through no fault of his own," he entered this world with so much stacked against him. As a child, when playing with others proved too boisterous, he would retreat to his Space Lego set which turned into a future passion.

Later, all I could think to say to her was, "Thank you for bringing this wonderful being into the world, for all the suffering your family endured." What I failed to acknowledge at the time was the evident mark of compassion carved also into the hearts of Bill's family…a quiet gentleness of being, woven into their lives. This is a priceless, costly gift beyond measure to humanity when the world becomes a brutal place.

This fierce love, conquering unspeakable odds, strengthened all of us through the remembrances of Bill's sister and his wife, enfolded in the haunting music of his son. A homemade spaceship, crafted by his young daughter, held a place of honour at the front...an aching reminder of all that had been taken...too soon, too soon... Still, it stood as a witness: the silent whisper God alone speaks into the mystery of Bill Heron's life... soaring at last into his 'wild blue yonder.' Signed, sealed, and delivered, he left his stamp on all of us.

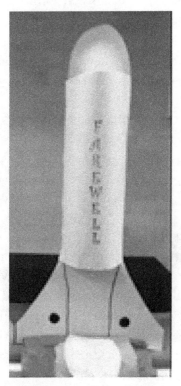

The Farewell Spaceship

Bill Heron

-JOYCE-

In the meantime, my sister, deep in weaving wreaths, had called again. Her husband's aunt, known to all of us as 'Aunt Joyce,' was a stalwart Salvation Army officer. Nearly 90, she had been 'Promoted to Glory.' Sometimes the mind just stalls. "Really, God, NOW?"

She too is part of the story of the lake, spending her retirement on her family's farm bordering the shore. She lived down the road from our cottage. Tall, elegant in her uniform, and with the title of Lieutenant Colonel, she was kind and solid in all of her ways. Her funeral, held after Christmas, takes place during an ice storm we cannot drive through. Part of me travels there anyway, to the church where I grew up... circa 1956.

The Salvation Army Hall is functional, plain, on a street ending at the water's edge. There are no stained-glass windows my heart always craved. The only splash of colour is the navy and blood-red flag with the yellow star in the middle..."The yellow, the red, and the blue."

The evening has gathered around us but we are safe within. The Christmas concert has come to its glorious conclusion. Our memorized parts have been remembered, at least most of them, delivered in fear and wonder. Miraculously, in memory, it has been a complete success as always.

Santa Claus has been spotted sailing through the navy-blue air...closer and closer he comes. The lights are dimmed. Suddenly, the door bursts open and there he is... my St. Nicholas, with bags of hard candy and gifts for all. We very nearly die. Then we are satisfied.

There is a scramble for coats and galoshes, a search for a missing woollen mitt, shouts of "See you in the morning! Look what I got!"Transported into Christmas Country, we are heading home... HOME.

TRANSITION

Lord, it feels like I am in a cave with no
way out, blocked by water. Suddenly, the
dam breaks and I'm rushing in the river,
grabbing, but there is nothing to grab.

Rebirthing.
Pushed into a glare of life I do not understand…

NEWBORN!

Sights and sounds I have never seen, never heard.

The familiar falls away.

"Where am I, Lord?"

"EVER WITH ME"

"Okay…then YES!

Just plant my feet on solid ground,
Wherever that ground may be.
Is this heaven, then?"

Joyce Ellery

Ember 5

"The Lord your God in your midst, The Mighty One,
will save; He will rejoice over you with
gladness,
He will quiet you with His love,
He will rejoice over you with singing."

Zephaniah 3:17
The New King James Version

- EPIPHANY -
- EPILOGUE -
-STAR -
- WISDOM-
-AFTERMATH-
-ROGUE WAVE-
- AUTHOR'S NOTE -

EPIPHANY

-ROSALIE-

Our porch light glowed as usual in the early evening hour, but next door, Cousin Rosalie's cottage was all in darkness, her car shrouded in snow. There was no friendly wave over the fence, no five-minute gabfest as we unpacked. There was only the silence of a soft January night.

Later, as we worked our way through 'the wake' into the room where so many of my family had rested in peace, my eyes were suddenly lifted from the closed casket to the screen above. Flashing pictures tell the story of 'this life well-lived'... Rosalie attempting to stand on a paddle board on our beloved lake...Rosalie golfing on all fours, figuring out the lay of the land ahead of her ball...Rosalie laughing beside a handsome young 'Elvis Presley.' (This small-town farm girl lived a large life from mission work in Romania to holidays in Panama.) Then, the circle of cousins, hugs all around, calls of "You made it!""Mom loved you so.""We'll get through this." All the things people say...

The next morning, there is one final gathering as we enter her Baptist church I haven't been in since childhood. (I suddenly remember a couple of weeks ago of having dreamt of this place, just a strange dislocated fragment of walking into this very sanctuary.) Last goodbyes are said as people shuffle by, juggling coats, hoping to get a seat. Then it all begins. How did we ever get to be here…a sudden October diagnosis, a visit in November… "You can beat this, Rosalie." A shocking descent, and now we are gathered together to celebrate her life.

Rosalie, this dedicated, efficient, and totally hilarious church lady whose sense of humour routinely set us off into gales of laughter, had of course chosen all the hymns. The first one,"I Cannot Tell,"[2]is set to the tune of"Danny Boy." At the best of times, this haunting melody manages to bring me to tears and I cannot sing. A powerful tenor voice behind me swells the notes, enveloping me in a memory that keeps returning to this day…words that speak of silence transforming into singing, darkness eclipsing in the light of heaven…the very power of resurrection. A great wave of strength soars up, pouring over me... a holy quickening of 'the unexpected joy.'

It isn't just the sparking of 20 years of blended summer memories. It is even greater than our collective childhood stories spanning back at least seven generations of family ties on this beloved lake. It is more than the remembrance of the blessed characters of 'The Shore…'when the water turns to lavender silver. Deeper, deeper still, it is the

---

[2] Paraphrased Personal Reflections inspired by"I Cannot Tell." Words: Ken Bible, inspired by William Y. Fullerton. Music: Traditional Irish Melody@1996 by LNWhymns.com. CCLI 21205

unquenchable hope for that which lays ahead... The Great Beginning.

The song crescendos us into one last hurrah of faith witnessing to a time beyond time, ushering all earthly flesh into the Essence of the Presence. The very seams of the sky break open, unable to withstand the power of the crashing waves of praise for the rising eternal Son... the dawning of the Saviour, now as Lord and King of this tattered world. In the midst of the now, we glimpse the joy set before us then.

Rosalie's faith had graduated to praise, as ours will one day. Until then, I found my voice belting out this last song with her, joining the heavenly choir, mingling with mortals. Afterwards, we did not linger. A January fog was fast setting in and we had miles to go. Rosalie had left the building. She had had her Easter day. "Joy comes in the morning."[3]

I have heard the angels sing.

---

[3]   Psalm 30:5, The New King James Version.

Rosalie Edgar

Epilogue

Home again from the lake, I half-heartedly pick up where I left off before all of this happened, beginning with The Tree. It is beyond time to undecorate and buckle down to January tasks. However, Master Procrastinator that I am, on go the lights still one more time.

My mind slips back to a faraway cold clear December night. Unthinkable now, I am walking home alone, in the dark, after our Sunday School concert practice. I like these moments to myself on the old familiar streets before returning to the pre-Christmas madness in any household full of siblings.

The sidewalk turns at what was the Livery Stable, a solid stone building now becoming a brewery. For the first time, the lights of the Spinner's Factory Christmas Tree come into view, both now long gone. If ever there was an awestruck moment in my life, it was then. Lost in the essence of childhood longing and expectation, "Joy inexpressible and full of glory"[4] flooded my soul. O Holy Night... O Come All Ye Faithful… O Little Town of Bethlehem… O…

---

[4] I Peter 1:8, The New King James Version.

Returning from my reverie to the task at hand, I begin packing away the familiar homemade red and silver candy canes, a shimmering angel, one golden star. Our tree is a hodgepodge of memories, triggering still another, coming back from a different time…

One of our nephews is attending college in a nearby city, and my husband and I have taken him to a Christmas Concert. There has been a family eruption of some sort, made worse by the December chaos of too much to do and not enough time to do it in.

Our nephew, Michael, is quietly aware that I am struggling with events. As we sit side by side, waiting for the concert to commence, he begins folding the paper program into different shapes. Quietly he forms a Christmas Star and gently, wordlessly, hands it to me. This sweet kindness I shall never forget, because it came with a reminder of God's presence and guidance to The Stable, the comfort of Emmanuel, Emmanuel, God with us, God with us. The next morning, this poem began to form. The eruption, whatever it was, ended. These words remained:

STAR

Step by step, I watched him fold the paper by design.
I could not follow as I watched the pattern in his mind.
But at the end he handed me a Christmas Star of white.
Then all the bends, the twist, the folds
Were gathered into light.

I lay all down upon the page of God's creative mind
And let Him bend and twist and
fold life's pattern by design.
Though what He makes I cannot see,
someday He'll hand to me
A golden star of perfect light to hang on heaven's tree…
All the while, His hands create this
Christmas Star for me.

I shall have to leave all of this in God's hands.

Under God's Wings,

Judy Imrie

WISDOM

"The souls of the just are in God's hand, and torment shall not touch them…in the moment of God's coming to them they will kindle into flame, like sparks that sweep through stubble. Those who have put their trust in Him shall understand that He is true and the faithful shall attend upon Him in love; they are His chosen, and grace and mercy shall be theirs."[5]

One ember glowing in the dark
To spark ten thousand candle flames.

-THE BEGINNING-

---

[5] Selected portions from The Wisdom of Solomon, Chapter 3:1-9, The Apocrypha, The New English Bible.

AFTERMATH

Grief ebbs, grief flows. 2020 passes into a pandemic and we are all living lives we could never have imagined. Rosalie's cottage has also passed into the hands of one of her daughters and grandchildren, Eve and Livy, and there is much future joy to contemplate in that continuance.

We arrive at the lake to check on our own. Mindful of the need to keep staying separate from others during these difficult days, we come prepared with groceries and all our necessities bought at home base. Being a natural-born introvert, I adapt to the quiet and the space to think my own thoughts. My more sociable husband struggles with the new rules of disengagement.

Feeling slightly bedraggled by the changes, especially the inability to visit our children and grandchildren, we catch the first news reports of the dreadful events unfolding in Nova Scotia. Beginning on a cottage road, not unlike our own, in a place called Portapique, comes a series of reports... murders, burnt-out homes, and charred remnants of police vehicles. 'The true North, strong and free' is brought to its knees. How could such a horror happen? If there, why not here? Another shadow of fear falls, joining forces with the dreaded COVID-19. In this place that has always been so full of such life, I feel violated by death.

We move through a few days of continued isolation to the televised Virtual Vigil for 22 proud Nova Scotians and one tiny unborn child. Homegrown and achingly beautiful, the songs and music touch the deep chords of loss hidden inside our own hearts. One in particular, "Light a Candle in the Window," causes me to do just that as I watch other lights spark around the shore. Disjointed phrases begin to form in my mind.

In the morning, an unfinished puzzle of 1000 broken pieces remains on a table in front of a window. The lighthouse of this puzzle lies finished, and the frame is complete, but there are huge gaps yet to fill in. I do not have the heart to begin... not yet. A tiny rainbow graces the wooden floor from light passing through a window hanging of coloured crystal teardrops. Placed to remember our niece, Margie, an effervescent memory of this 'force of nature' suffuses the room. Elusive words spark around the darkened edges of my mind.

We keep meaning to leave, not having intended to stay very long. "Not yet, not yet. Stay the course," a silent whisper breathes. This blessed place holds us here and so we stay. One morning we wake to a cruel northeast wind. It batters the cottage all day long, whipping the waves into a frenzy of cross-action.

On this dark overcast day, with supplies running low, I clear the final supper here for now. Absentmindedly looking out, I am astonished by the sudden appearance of a perfect half-circle of golden sunshine, a horseshoe, a hug, edging all around the lower trees and cottages of our bay. Above this, I also trace the faintest of rainbows gracing the sky. We have stayed 'for such a time as this.' A poem, also edging around the corners of my mind for days, finally locks together, snapping puzzling emotions coherently into place. The words, at last, pour out on paper. Next morning we pack to leave.

The lake ebbs, the lake flows.

ROGUE WAVE

It comes, it comes, caught in the corner of an eye.
It grows, it grows…
Its shadow settles on the mind.
It rises, rises, falling on the shore…
This Jonah Whale.

It swallows, swallows in its dreadful wake.
It takes, it takes
And we are all displaced.
But then it stops, it dissipates.
The morning dawns for Goodness' Sake.

We wake, unfurl, to rise again.
We scan the shore in disbelief.
Then from the corner of an eye…
a glimpse, a trace, an edge of light,

One touch of grace,
A rainbowed sky,
Sweet Breathing Space.

Love comes to swallow up the grief
Enfolding us in arms of peace
And we are blessed.

Under God's Wings,

Judy Imrie

AUTHOR'S NOTE
Cardinal View Cottage
August 7, 2020

On the 5th of February 2020, what began as a letter of condolence to Eve and Livy evolved into the nearly 10,000 preceding words. I hope it honours the 'Sparks' of the story whose families have graciously allowed me to share these remembrances with a wider audience. Grief can be intensely private, and I appreciate their openness to help others on the same path. Sometimes, in the telling of stories, grief is relieved. May yours be also as you tell you own.

There are times many of us go through a series of surreal experiences that seem to have no ending. During more than one particular season, this became true for our extended family and our community along with ourselves. Personally, on those occasions, I was left stunned by the storm of my own emotions… profound anger when, in the blink of an eye, all of a sudden, before you know it... life becomes 'so NOT the way it is supposed to be.' COVID-19 has brought the world to this.

Several years before any of these painful events took place, my husband and I were sight seeing at the base of Grouse Mountain in British Columbia. He decided to take the gondola ride up to the top which I refused to do.

Mountains in my view are best enjoyed from the bottom. However, it became apparent he was planning dinner for us at the revolving restaurant perched in the clouds. Never one to miss a meal under any circumstances, I finally acquiesced.

After a successful landing and with all fear forgotten, we lingered late over our meal. The brilliant view of Vancouver Harbour at sunset was mesmerizing, and at one point, the horizon seemed to melt entirely away, leaving ships suspended in the sky itself. The line between heaven and earth disappeared, swallowed in the peace of that evening.

Years later, that very same profound image would return to my mind's eye when I needed it most. However, this time, superimposed over this 'memory photo,' several cocoons 'appeared.'(Spaced separately in thin air, we would now call it social distancing.) They arrived with the assurance that there is a time and a place for solitude when the wounds are too raw for others to touch… 'emotional burn units' to be inhabited… but only for a time until grief could be shared and the pain of another acknowledged and softened. Therein lies our saving grace.

A calmness came with that, an acceptance that grief is neither right nor wrong. It just is. Loss of any kind comes with an individual reaction with a healing time as diverse as humankind itself. My first response to calamity will probably always be anger, and that is the cocoon I will battle against leaving the longest. However, cocoons were never meant to be permanent habitations either. In the meantime, while God enfolds us in our lonely spaces, 'give it time, Butterfly, give it time.'

That picture of safe harbour returning to grace my mind became a comfort. Behind the necessary cocoons, the 'brilliant view' remained. It grew stronger with focus kept until it was time to emerge. Sometimes we have to 'climb a mountain' to see the bigger picture or go back to the lake. This is where I am this morning, watching the sun crack open another summer's day, dancing on the surface of the bay...

May Comfort and Joy come to you
also, some gentle morning.

Judy

For the Lord shall comfort Zion: he
will comfort all her waste places;
and he will make her wilderness like
Eden and her heart like the
garden of the Lord; joy and gladness
shall be found therein;
thanksgiving and the voice of melody.

Isaiah 51:3

After a terrible time,
"There was great joy in that city."

Acts 8:8
The King James Version

About the Author

When the lake turns to lavender silver at Cardinal View Cottage, seven generations of family stories rise with the campfire smoke. Writing for Judy Imrie is the natural outcome of sharing memories and triggering them in others. It soothes the soul in the middle of the wonderful circus of family life, including an entrepreneur husband of fifty-one years, two loving daughters and their husbands along with four amazing grown grandchildren. Golden Retrievers, Benjamin and William, and the star of the family, Norman the Pug, are a constant source of inspiration and joy for this author.

A background in health care for over thirty years as a coder in Health Records while participating in several family businesses has been interspersed with travel and Anglican Church activities. Writing to encourage and bring laughter into the world remains at the core of Judy's reason for sharing these stories and poems.

CPSIA information can be obtained
at www.ICGtesting.com
Printed in the USA
BVHW030800111120
592860BV00021B/20